Sassing

Sassing

Poems by Karen Head

WordTech Editions

Published by WordTech Editions
P.O. Box 541106
Cincinnati, OH 45254-1106

ISBN: 9781934999592
LCCN: 2009928723

Poetry Editor: Kevin Walzer
Business Editor: Lori Jareo

Visit us on the web at www.wordtechweb.com

for my parents

Table of Contents

Hester Speaks

1.

Listen child,
to what you imagine I know
to memories you do not have—
me lying beside Settindown Creek
before the cotton mill's wheel
began churning the water
before the white man
stole me from the past
and built the covered bridge
before I was old enough
to know my Cherokee name
formed from dancing spirits
that call me on the wind.

2.

Even without memory,
I knew I should never
cut my hair—
so I grew it past the hips
that birthed a line to you
kept it in two tight braids
I would tie together
across my waist
the ends hanging loose
between my legs
thickly woven, separate lives.

3.

I do not remember
how I learned
to dance
a cup and saucer
filled with well-water
balanced on my head
how I managed
not to spill anything
why I did it the first time
why I continued.

4.

My Christian name
was a mistake
a misspelling of Esther,
another foreign bride.
She knew her real name—
Hadassah was careful
about revealing herself
but had memories, choices—
I did not marry a king
could not save my people.

5.

When you dance, child,
do you feel me?
I've watched you
spin wildly
unafraid
unashamed
unaware
it is me you hear,
my cup tipping over,
whispering a new name
for the rhythms
you cannot resist.

I

"Years ago we in the South made our women into ladies. Then the War came and made the ladies into ghosts"
—Mr. Compson in Faulkner's *Absalom, Absalom!*

"The biggest myth about Southern women is that we are frail types—fainting on our sofas...nobody where I grew up ever acted like that. We were about as fragile as coal trucks."
—Lee Smith

Part of the Bargain

"Take a shiny quarter for it?"
She clutched my left ring finger
caressing the wart I wanted rid of.
She had an eye twitch
as if a rapid wink had possessed her.
I couldn't imagine why
this old crone would want my wart
how exactly she would get it,
but I was thirteen and desperate,
tired of the cute boys, ugly ones too,
saying I was out kissing frogs,
calling me a witch.
So, when Granny offered
to sneak me over to the conjure woman
while my mama was running errands
I was game, eager even,
just didn't realize I'd be selling
a part of myself.

Standing there on that back porch
overhanging a creek,
I could hear the croaking
as I took the quarter
and one last look at my wart.
"Belongs to me now, quit your looking."
Her eye no longer twitched.
She turned back into her shack,
and Papa drove us home.

Next day, the wart was gone
and for the first time in my life
I felt I'd sold out,
gave away my magic for nearly nothing.

Southern Gothic

The best I can offer
is that my granny and papa
lived on a dead-end dirt road
in a single-wide trailer,

that one of Daddy's sisters
accidentally drank rat poison
stored in an old green wine jug
after a night of cards and drinking,

that Mama and Daddy married,
sixteen and eighteen,
three weeks into his Army Basic Training
and no baby came for over a year,

that I was born on Peachtree Street—
Crawford Long Hospital, Atlanta, Georgia
six weeks early, four pounds,
nothing but wailing,

that I was baptized outside
Mt. Pisgah Baptist Church,
then blacklisted from membership
when I became a Catholic.

My life has been full of movement
one Army base to another—
opera in Stuttgart
schnapps at a Mississippi levee.

Hell, for me, has two syllables
and I'm always fixin' to do something
so, you can imagine my surprise
when the doctor said, "Lupus,"

and I realized what was finally at my door.

Military Wife

"If you have any more children, you will die."
My brother's tiny hand wrapped
around my mother's index finger.
Staring into the doctor's eyes—
only seventeen, in a foreign country—
she agreed to have her tubes tied.

Ten years later they told her,
"Impossible!"
She dug her heels into the stirrups.
In America, she would not acquiesce.
Death almost took her.
With no recollection of my birth,
she was sent home alone
forced to leave me in an incubator
with those same nay-saying doctors.

I never suckled,
did not see my mother's breasts
until I was fairly grown,
until they sagged weighted
under years of being told *no*.

My mother never went to college,
did not have a public career.
She married at fifteen,
exhausting her individuality
somewhere between

the smoldering ruins of Atlanta
and a base near the Berlin Wall.
She was a good wife, a good mother.
But lately when I stare hard at her face,
I notice she is old.

When I encourage her to try new things
she smiles—her eyes glaze.
A couple of years ago she said,
"I don't think you will ever have children;
I want you to know I'm okay with that."
When I first began college, I didn't talk much,
thought she wouldn't understand.
Now, every morning, over coffee,
she telephones and I tell her
everything I learned the day before.

Elizabeth Retreats

after Fred Chappell

No one here is of a proper age
To understand Elizabeth at this stage
When all that's good is past or yet to come

Surely, Fred, we must be related.
My Yankee friends think we are *all* related,
talk slow, marry our cousins,
but what about you and me,
the ones who got *edge-u-cated*?

Off in our universities, we write poems
about aunts, grannies, cousins and such,
paint them eccentric, crazy—
us, but not us.

At family gatherings, my kin-folk
keep asking, "You done with school?"
They don't understand who I am—
they know me better than I know myself,
still send me off to the porch
where I eavesdrop on their world.

I know your niece, Elizabeth,
she's me, I'm her,
dancing blind in the half-light
determined to hear and not hear
the voices from within,
cradled in the porch-swing
dreaming gibberish
I'm learning to translate.

Aesthetics

When I was a little girl,
I used to make mud-cakes
in dented, aluminum ice-trays.
The art was deciding exactly
the combination of dirt and water.
Something about the presentation
never seemed quite right—
the mud framed by
an occasional glint of silver
not worn from years of ice
scraping over the sides.
The scent of old-fashioned
climbing roses beckoned me
to the backyard fence—
I would pluck blossoms with abandon,
nicking the tips of my white fingers
on the tiny, almost hidden thorns.
Then I would carefully separate the petals
arranging them as icing for my cakes,
with tiny dots of blood as sprinkles.

Southern Girls

wear a hat on Derby Day,
swoon over Elvis, still
drink tea with too much sugar
fix their man's supper plate
stand by relatives' graves
Easter Sun Rise Service,
know how to shell peas
fire a shotgun
own a pressure cooker
tend azaleas
talk slow
bake squash casseroles
for mourning neighbors,
sneak-sip moonshine
never wear pants to church
eat grits
hickory-switch their children
country music two-step
get baptized outside
are buried in rose-covered
pink satin-lined coffins,
no matter how poor,
drag their vowels and smile
when they sass

Economy

My grandmother spent her life saving.
She would take me into her gardens, teach me
to clip and re-root almost dead plants,
burn paper trash to mix in vegetable beds,
tear old dish rags to secure tomatoes.

She lived through The Depression—lucky to be on a farm.
Her father had shared food with starving city relatives.
There were always leftovers warming in her oven.
"Ain't no sense wasting this," she would say,
letting me lick white fudge frosting from her mixing bowl.
When she began to toss out things,
I knew there was a problem.
Then she began to forget recipes, didn't water her plants,
couldn't even hold onto my name.

A Short History of Georgia

My ancestors were the other Georgians—
not the aristocratic Brits landed in Savannah,
the ones who would build columned plantations,
but the Scots-Irish hardscrabble farmers,
debtor-prison parolees, and a Cherokee girl.

Great-grandfathers on both sides wore Rebel gray,
but didn't fall by Yankee hands, didn't venture
far from the Blueridge foothills. Then there were farmers
and cotton-mill workers, who survived Restoration
and the Depression, not noticing much difference.

Great thinkers, nostalgic, have told the story
of the ideal South, about simplicity—
the Agrarian utopia. They chose to ignore how
the New South is not so different from the Old,
how the land cannot resurrect the people.

I am one of the first in my family to attend college—
a graduate of Oglethorpe, named for Georgia's founder,
where I first read Faulkner, first understood fury and sound
and why Caddy could not speak for herself—
where I first realized how much I had to say.

Grandmother's Spit
after Andrew Hudgins

She catches you by the collar or belt loop
pulls you back, spins you around, grabs shoulders
plants you firmly in front of her.
It is the price you pay for licking the bowl,
taking the short cut through the pasture,
or playing baseball with cherry tomatoes.
For the boys, it always seems so quick:
the spit, the rub, the bolt for the back of the trailer,
the wiping away begun before they turn the corner.
As a girl, I know different.
First, there will be the sweeping back of hair,
the clothing readjusted and the reprimands
about how young ladies should act.
Finally, the matrilineal baptism, snuff & butter scented,
the thickness clinging to my face, Granny eyeing me,
until I collapse beside her, folding my hands in my lap.

For Show

You always see them in guest half-baths
sitting in small frosted crystal dishes
next to the gardenia-scented potpourri
and the embroidered finger towels—
those tiny carved soaps—
pastel faux seashells or roses.
You never actually touch them,
don't even notice the dust
settled into crevices
the owner tries to brush away
each time she hosts a party.
Upstairs in the master bath,
with the green bar soap
and the tattered, once white, washcloth
stained from makeup and blood,
she makes herself pretty for the guests
who will say how nice things look.

Exhibitions

"I've never seen a real pig,"
I said, trying to piece together
the farmyard puzzle from Grandma.
Two weeks later my father surprised me
with a trip to the state fair.
My favorites were the baby ducks,
swimming around their narrow moat.
They climbed the steps to a dangling feeder,
leaned their tiny beaks forward,
then slid down the little ramp,
splash, back into the moat.

Thirty years later,
I lean over the side
of the giant Ferris-wheel,
watch the people below mill about
eating corn-dogs and funnel cakes.
I look up at the flashing lights
and think of the animals in their pens,
pigs, sheep, cows, horses,
and the ducks, still plunging
for that single kernel.

Georgia Clay

It was quite a common sight to see a group of women
gathered on the porch sharing a plate of dirt.
—Dr. Dennis Frate

In my grandparents' pine-thicket
there was an open space, depressed,
where water would pool in spring,
dry-up in summer, cracked ground
as if hundreds of broken red plates
had been tossed in a pile.
Linda and I would play tea party,
arrange a table on the grass,
azalea blooms at each fractured setting.
Some days we would dig deeper
find real treasure—
white clay, kaolin
soft as cheese for imaginary crackers.
Once, my granny watched me
pretend to nibble,
"Stop it! That's what poor women do."
I dug small holes, buried the white chalk,
then sucked my marked fingers,
discovered the sweet bitterness of earth.

II

SIREN, n. One of several musical prodigies famous for a vain attempt to dissuade Odysseus from a life on the ocean wave. Figuratively, any lady of splendid promise, dissembled purpose and disappointing performance.
—Ambrose Bierce, *The Devil's Dictionary*

Light My Fire
1967

Coltrane died the week I was born.
Sheets of sound pulled too tight
for me to hear outside the incubator walls,
as if in an empty theatre
I arrived too early to the show,
still missed him—
just missed his expression
the stellar regions of *altissimo*
audible only to dogs and babies.
In the spiritual shrill, I wailed after him,
wanted to leave before I'd really come,
but the nurse cranked the radio by her desk
and the lizard king callously crooned,
"The time to hesitate is through
no time to wallow in the mire...
come on baby,"
                              and so I did.

Grazing in the Grass
1968

before language there is music
voices are just accompaniment
that float in baby's ears
nothing but melodies and harmony
hovering over the crib
adults cling to infancy
lose track of lyric
cooing, babbling, for the comfort
of the child—they think—
or don't think, for a change
until slowly the pattern evolves
and music gives way
to the first staccato words—"Mama," "Dada"
and "No!"

In the Year 2525
1969

Thirteen generations from now
there will be no line of children's
children's children,
no child to remember
me.

At two, I do not know this
but by the twenty-first century
when saying two thousand
seems banal, simple,
I will have learned about DNA
mitosis
periods
bad one-liners
wham bam thank you ma'am's
divorce
menopause
and empty wombs,
when words are all I have to bequeath.

Close to You
1970

My red tricycle
with wide black wheels
scuffed the walls
from living room
to back bedroom.
I'm not sure where
I thought I was going.
An indoor racetrack.

When I hit the walls
maybe it wasn't lack of control
but my first attempts to break out
still catching on the umbilical cord,
a jet landing on an aircraft carrier
speeding forward until the cable stops it
until I turn around and fly off again.

Indian Reservation
1971

Great great-grandmother Hester could dance
a saucer of water on her head
the price of not having a price
having been stolen by a God-fearing
Scots Irish Georgia mountain man
whose sons would march with Lee
always someone having to march
having to trail behind history and fear.

I have her Cherokee cheekbones.
When I was only four
I even had a single feather headband
I wore over long dark braids.
My brother would shoot at me
with his Lone Ranger cap pistol
march me around the yard
until naptime, when I dreamed of dancing.

Lean on Me
1972

Kindergarten, Pioneer Barracks, Hanau, West Germany

Independence is easy at five,
no real fear of anything,
getting lost maybe,
but the world still seems small.
The day school let out early and Mom forgot,
the van left me and a neighbor boy
at the corner bus-stop.

The mother deep inside me,
the mother I'd never really be,
grabbed the tufted haired boy,
so small for his age,
clutched his hand and began walking
pulling him along as he cried,
wanting to cry, wanting to hurry,
wanting to the turn the corner—
find my way home.

Living in the Material World
1973

Most important was my Flintstones' lunchbox
pink metal canvas for Pebbles
also in pink, like my first-day dress
trimmed in eyelet tatting on the hem and sleeves.
Girls still couldn't wear pants,
but the teachers could paddle us,
and on the playground
I learned about the cool girls
who had their Dick and Jane readers
covered in flower-power contact paper,
mine wrapped in recycled grocery bags
harder to read out loud
sitting in the language arts circle,
Montclair Elementary, First Grade.

Annie's Song
1974

The cool kid in second grade
wasn't me, but I got to sit
neatly in a row with others
out of reach of Annie, who hit

so many times, she'd been exiled
to a desk outside arm's reach
of any other student,
right beside our teacher.

On Valentine's day,
we hung pouches, heart shaped,
along the bottom of the blackboard,
ate candy hearts until our bellies ached,

but the real ache was watching Annie
check her pouch over and again
only finding one from Mrs. Miller.
In second grade, we'd learned to sin,

already shunning girls like Annie.
My mother had made me sign cards
for every student in class, but one
never made it past the schoolyard.

The Hustle
1975

"Just watch American Bandstand,"
my brother said as he packed his duffel bag.
I wasn't sure how I could learn to dance
watching a television show
but for once I was trying
not to be a pesky little sister.

On the way to the Greyhound Station
he didn't try to commandeer
the entire backseat, didn't pinch me,
or offer me a dollar to lie in the floor-well
so he could stretch out, be comfortable.
He tapped his foot to a silent beat
while we waited to say goodbye.

Over Burger King Whoppers and shakes,
we talked about how funny he'd look in uniform.
At home, when I didn't feel well,
Daddy told me not to bother my mother.
I found her crying in the bathroom,
bent double on the toilet seat.
"You're just sad because your brother's gone,"
she told me, shutting the door.

Next morning, I woke to a terrible itch,
pained to the bone, delirious from fever.
Mom forgot some of her sadness,
consumed as much as I was
by Chicken Pox.
I didn't think about dancing for a week,
until Saturday came without any music
from Mickel's room.

Mom fixed the couch as a sick bed,
turned the TV dial until she found what I wanted—
Dick Clark surrounded by dozens of kids
about my brother's age,
lined up like a phalanx,
all of them dancing alone.

Kiss and Say Goodbye
1976

The first guitar player I ever loved
was my fourth grade music teacher,
who wore faded jeans, a pony-tail,
smelled of musk and cigarettes.
When the other teachers were absent
he let us call him Eddie: very cool.
Every girl in class giggled
when he took our hands,
repositioned fingers on frets.
We were groupies
before we could imagine
the meaning of the word.

Sherry and Lynn,
whose daddies outranked mine,
both blonde, wore the newest fashions,
could do the splits in gym class,
were used to having their way.
On the playground, they would whisper
loud enough for me to hear,
"He won't pick her to be teacher's helper.
She isn't pretty enough."

When Eddie finally picked me,
I tried to get even, gave the girls
the dreaded tuba and bassoon.
They whimpered until he went to them—
the first man to leave me
at the back of the room
clutching his guitar.

Looks Like We Made It
1977

Nellingen Kaserne, West Germany

My first kiss took
three weeks, two days, seven hours.
It could have happened anywhere:
underneath the playground slide,
behind the roller rink,
in the shadow of the medivac heliport.
I was afraid of getting caught.
The only glamorous part
was that it was in Germany—
next to France where, I'd heard,
kissing was different.
He leaned against the banister,
on the first step going to the basement,
just a gray, cinderblock stairwell.
We had to whisper because of the echo.
He tasted like lemon-drops.
His name was David.
It would never again be so simple.

Shadow Dancing
1978

The silver studded bellbottom jeans
my mother ordered from the Sears Catalog
did not arrive in time for my first dance.
Embarrassed by my boys-cut Levis,
I was afraid Troy or David or Scott
would only see their kick-ball buddy.

The Base Youth Facility
actually owned a small mirror ball
to twirl stars around constellations
of pre-teens, arranged by gender,
always a few wall-flower moons,
orbiting the dance floor.

The chaperones drafted some real teens
from their pinball game, to show us
how to dance; they thought we were shy.
What we really needed to know was when
we should stop wiggling in place—
begin to reach for each other.

Bad Girls
1979

Two of the town's three steel mills were closed
before we arrived, fresh from Europe,
the new post sergeant major and his family.

The Saint Louis Army Depot is actually in Illinois.
Mississippi-downstream from the Alton refineries—
a place people try to leave.

Prather Junior High backed up to the highway
faced a dilapidated rooming house
at the end of a closed-off street.

Most students came early for free breakfast
stayed more for the free lunch than for learning
never seemed anxious to get home.

No wonder the Depot kids seemed rich.
We wore a few of the season's fashions
bought from a mall thirty miles away.

Gwen's father was a lieutenant-colonel
monied even by military standards.
She was impeccable in French braids and Izod.

A target really, with pink and green satin ribbons.
Sandy, wearing St. Vincent DePaul jeans
couldn't help but hate delicate Gwen.

I was the new girl when I met them both.
The air between them already soured
by nothing either could understand.

I admired Sandy's strength,
coveted Gwen's grace,
did not know which one I wanted more.

When I saw Gwen pushed down
Sandy gripping her braids
to drag her down the hall

I stepped between them.
It must have been the sheer shock of me
that momentarily linked us—

so weary of who we were trying to be.

It's Still Rock and Roll to Me
1980

Two summers earlier, mom went nuts
when I had asked her to sign me up for softball,
saying no one cared about her feelings.
Mom's best friend, Mrs. Caffey, laughed,
hysterical, when I told her what happened,
she gave me cookies and said some day I'd understand.
My father sent us stateside for a few weeks.

I'd only had my period for three years
when my mother began to lose hers,
bleeding for weeks, until the doctor said, "Enough!"

Mom was in the hospital, and my cheerleading
uniform was still in the hamper.
I didn't know about washing machine pipes
being so old that the water had to be turned off
after each use—too easy to knock out
the drain hose. I flooded the kitchen,
and my father just handed me a mop,
walked away without saying a word.

I've had my period for almost thirty years.
still can't imagine it ending—each month
I rinse out my panties, splash water on the floor.

The One that You Love
1981

I knew he loved me when he busted
the dashboard engine light
with a screwdriver
to save me from
the too bright, red glow
illuminating my unbuttoned
unzipped, untouched
before this moment, body

outside the frigid April night
caused the windows to fog
pop love poured from the radio
we struggled to discover
the mystery of how bodies
feel different without cover
butted against the glove compartment
he rose above me with the
vinyl seat of that 74 Granada
sticking me in place
afterwards, when I cleaned up
with a fast food napkin,
all I could recall
was the vacancy sign
on the motel we couldn't afford

driving home
I traced a heart on the window
then wiped it with my forearm
so he could see to turn on the highway
we made curfew
early even
but were too guilty to kiss
under the porch light

Eye of the Tiger
1982

Killing my father
crossed my mind once:
when he pronounced his Army retirement.
It was a surprise attack,
his years in combat
an advantage. He cornered
us in the dining room.
All those years of world travel over—
a final relocation to rural Georgia.
It was the end
of my freshman year of high school.
I was in love with Tommy.
I was going to be on the yearbook staff.
I had to move.
My mother was no help.
She leaned against the doorframe,
stared down at my father's boots,
sighed as she shook her head.
I fired killer looks,
knowing it was too late
for death to save me.

Every Breath You Take
1983

Homeroom felt like a crowded elevator
cables stressed beyond capacity
traveling down too fast.
I imagined everyone laughing
dropped my books, backed out,
Ms. Aparo called after me.
I ran to the counselors' office,
said what I'd been saying for weeks,
"Please help me!"
When the same answer came,
"You're a smart girl, a good head
on your shoulders. No worries."
I began to scream. Pulled books
from shelves, toppled a table—
the secretary phoned my mother.

I told the psychologist the story,
how I'd helped Joey
find Kim the perfect birthday gift—
how he hadn't invited me to the party
so I'd stayed home that Saturday—
how I couldn't believe my parents
had brought me to this hick town—
how these civilian kids
didn't need any new friends—
how I was so tired of trying—
how being smart could not make sixteen sweet.

When Doves Cry
1984

I wrote you bad poetry, teenage poems
about how I was cotton, would be silk,
would grow up, become a woman who could
make you the happiest man in the world.
At seventeen, I thought love was all you
needed to be powerful, to be whole.
Opening night of the spring play, I pinned
a white carnation to your suit lapel
and you smiled, called me a frail butterfly.
You never said goodbye, left me standing
alone in the quiet of the classroom.
The new teacher would be younger, handsome,
but I would not sing for him, did not know
how my luck with men would echo from you.

A View to a Kill
1985

I've blocked all the memories
the ones that made me fall for you,
but I do remember the day we met—
you were standing in the service garage
a tire iron under your left arm
greasy fingers fumbling yellow work orders
some guy yelling about his unbalanced tires.
You walked into your office
slammed the door and the wall.
I also recall an early date
the one when you held my head down
pushed your cock into my mouth,
but when the explosion hit the back of my throat
it came right back, along with my dinner,
onto your lap, onto the seats of your new car.
That was the first time you called me a bitch,
the first time I failed to clean up our mess.

Sledgehammer
1986

In the wedding photos
I look like baby-bride-Barbie,
my hair in tight French braids,
white lace ruffles, seventy-two buttons
running down my back
to satin ballerina shoes.

The day I came home
to find my stuffed bunny,
hanging from a noose
tied to the bedroom ceiling fan—
flap   flap   flap—
That's the day I should have left.

The last day we were together
he hammered his ring flat
threw it off the balcony.
For once, he didn't hit me
only smashed crystal and china
ripped out wedding album pages.
I remember laughing—
when I crossed the threshold.
I was wearing jeans and hiking boots.

Alone
1987

The day my divorce was final
I woke up in another man's bed,
rushed home, changed clothes
went downtown to the courthouse.

The last thing my husband said to me:
"You'll regret leaving me,
no other man will have you."
He was wrong. And right.

III

"Twenty years from now you will be more
disappointed by the things that you didn't do
than by the ones you did do."
    —Mark Twain

"Dreams, if they're any good, are always a little crazy."
    —Ray Charles

Autumn Rain

Sounds like applause—
not the kind you hear
center-stage, crowds roaring,
but the same sound
as it ricochets off the bricks
that separate the theatre
and the bar next door
where you sit alone
waiting for someone,
or something, not coming.

Shadow Boxes

In a box, in the upstairs closet at my parent's house,
are photographs taken before I was born.

The sepia-prints, with gold-green hues, are surreal
painted versions of the parents I know.

By the time I met them, they were more settled,
past their carefree twenties.

My parents were not hippies, so these photos are
their only tie-dyed relics.

Some of the photos have blood soaked edges,
from being in my father's wallet when the car-jack

gave way and crushed his leg in Panama.
But that didn't save him from going to Vietnam.

My mother smiling, looks serene and beautiful,
with that halo of brownish-red, encircling her head,

as if waiting for my father, four-times she waited,
to return from the lush jungle

of camouflage green, and gun-metal gray,
with fogs of agent-orange blocking out the sun.

On Visiting Duane Allman's Grave
Macon, Georgia

A crisp spring Sunday afternoon
Rose Hill Cemetery
we walk along the railroad tracks
climb the ravine to where he rests.

A train slides down the tracks
its steady, steely, screeching
accompanies our silent staring
as a bittersweet echo fills our mind's ear.

A full fret glide on a slide guitar
the sensual, slick sonority—
a Harley careening out of control
shifting, squealing, slipping away—

Writing on Napkins

in response to David Bottoms

The platinum blonde brought you a Pabst Blue Ribbon,
her hair the color of beer sweat on a frosty mug,
blue powder in waves on her eyelids,
of course she wants to think you're writing love letters
because that's better than you writing her sentimental.
She doesn't want be bothered with a poet.
It's just you've been in that booth all night
and she's looking for a good tip.
You do have the brunette at the pinball machine right;
her belch is something real,
something more like a Hank Williams song,
in tune enough to let her body sound,
ricochet off the no-tilt bells and whistles,
the kind of woman who knows without thinking.

Legacy

Shelling purple hulls and long white runners
I watched my grandfather rock under the dogwood tree.
Shining a buck-eye, he explained it would bring me luck.
More interested in his stories than his advice,
I was too young to realize they were one and the same.
His teeth gone for years and false ones on a shelf,
he could still eat corn on the cob and smile.
He learned to live without obstructions,
said things were simpler that way,
showed he loved me by offering a stick of Juicy-Fruit.
I popped it in my mouth,
the sweetness lingering a lifetime.

The Only Time I've Seen My Daddy Cry

Granny Head sang at her own funeral.
I was sitting next to my father
when my cousin, Janette,
the gospel singer, took the pulpit.
We thought she was gonna sing,
but she told a story instead:
Granny had gone
to the recording studio
not long before she died,
a little outing, with the tape rolling.

I can't remember the song
that came from the funeral home speakers—
just my Granny giggling when she'd finished.

Still Life

Precariously held by a magnet to the filing cabinet next to my desk, is a photo of my grandparents. One of their last public appearances together, they are dressed up in Sunday-go-to-meeting clothes, like when the preacher showed up late, wearing overalls, and married them on my great-grandparents' front porch. They seem oblivious to the camera. On their wedding night they went to the picture show, 1934. Once I asked what the movie was, but they grinned and said they didn't remember. When they were courting, my grandfather had a wandering eye, so when he finally proposed, Granny made him wait seven months before agreeing. He didn't want to leave her that night in 1997, her Alzheimer's so bad she clung to his hand like a child. My whole life I only heard her call him Papa, but that night she whispered his name, over and over, like a question. "Cliff?"

May Day Sermon
in response to James Dickey

"Listen O daughters turn turn"

No, not May.
Not hot enough for fiery conversions.
It was late July.
The smell of chicken houses drifting through the open
        windows,
the church piano, strings stressed atonal,
popsicle stick advertising fans flapping off beat
one side Christ night cooled in the shade of Gethsemane
the other side the new porch at Ingram's funeral parlor.
It was a Friday, and I was just days short of sixteen.

His name was Bobby, and he would leave in another year
off to engineering school   his mind always
        full of pure science
but tonight, his curiosity had excited my mama into
        believing
that there might finally be a good Christian boy in my
        future.

It would only be a matter of weeks before a future
        film student
would come back from Texas , the summer with his father,
full of mystery beyond anything I'd found in church,
complete with his jazz shoes that made everybody

think he was gay.
I would choose him over Bobby for my homecoming date
and his car would break down, and we wouldn't get
our photo made at the dance
and after I drove him home in my mother's car he
would ask if I wanted to fool around
and I would say no.   A few years later, we'd
have the same conversation,
and he would show me his journal where he wrote
that he dreamed I was on fire
and the entry would be on the same date my ex-
husband dosed me with developing fluid
and again I would say no.

So, here I was with Bobby in a whitewashed,
          clapboard, country church
during summer revival, and the three preachers had
          been at it for hours
and everyone was singing:
          Just as I am without one plea
and the preacher was waving his arms in the air and
          bellowing,
          Come, sinner, come home.
and that's when it happened.
Wanda, a church matron, spied Bobby and made a
          bee-line for him.
          *Boy, do you know the Lord Jesus Christ as your
          eternal savior?*
Bobby glanced over his shoulder at me and I tried to say,
          Run!

The next thing I knew he was up front, down on his knees,
and I couldn't get near him because there was a circle
          of folks praying over him.
All I could think was get me out of here.
          I wanted to scream,
          He's a Unitarian.
But I choked on an old time silence.
All I could feel was my own baptism,
in the mossy concrete pool out back of the church
filled every summer by the local fire department
Brother Morgan pushing me under,
my dress pinned between my legs so it wouldn't float up.

Then the preacher hollered at Bobby,
          Give your heart over to the Lord, son.
Eventually, they gave up when Bobby couldn't see
          what they wanted him to see
and when we drove home, he laughed, but I just
          wanted to cry.
We fooled around for a few weeks, but it never got
          past third,
and then I dumped him out of pure shame.

Brother Jim, you know damn well there ain't any
          women preachers in Gilmer County
and even if there were, they wouldn't have to warn
          young women about lust and murder
and riding off into the night, naked on a motorcycle,
          man between their knees.
Because that night late in July during my sixteenth

year, I was just one county over
just a few years past my own drowning and the new
          dry dress for the photos
and I could tell you then what I know for sure now
you don't need your daddy to string you up in a barn
          to beat the sin out of you
because the sin swirls like a spring tornado from the
          moment you gasp into this world
and the only thing that separates men and women is
          that the women know
that neither love nor God can save you from some things.

Service
for MK

"When you're ready," she said, placing her beer on the table,
"you will find the strength to air it." Dirty linen for an
     ordered table.

At the Trappist monastery, I'm afraid to write in my cell,
pace the grounds, wait for the monks to set the table.

It's the silent sobbing, the loneliness, I don't want to
     remember,
the evenings when he hammered my skull against the
     coffee-table.

I prayed for God to help me, considered the afterlife,
believed I had nowhere to go, no one to invite me to
     their table.

The false sense of helplessness is the greatest abuser.
Incoherent, I reconfigured my life based on a faulty
     amortization table.

I never calculated the real rate of interest—the time
     that will never heal
the unmeasured, unrelenting ache—the memory I
     cannot table.

"When you are ready…" my head begins to pound.
Do I acquit the villain by keeping this under the table?

Ella's Diner

Sitting at the counter, I notice the old woman, her
heel catching on the doorframe as she wrestles her
large, orange swing coat from the wind, crying
"Haaay Jessie! Gimme some HOT coffee." I hadn't
noticed the waitress's name emblazoned on a doily-
backed napkin, pinned against her sagging breast. The
old woman has skin the color of gingerroot that
her lime-green dress does not flatter. She is a regular.

I keep eating my hashbrowns, trying not to stare.
"You awful spry to be wasting your time in a joint like
this." Jessie taps a spoon on the counter to get my
attention. "Excuse me, ma'am?" "Ma'am? Lord, you
are green. Name's Mahellya." I swallow a sip of my
Coke, "Nice to meet you Miss Mahalia." She creases
her eyes, correcting me, "Not Mawhalyah, more like
ma hell same as ya, just without the same as in the
middle." Jessie snickers.

"So what man done drove you out to a greasy spoon
this time of night?" I feel like a rotten-looking potato
left unharvested, with its one good, hidden eye facing
down in the fertile soil. I had just begun to take root
when she discovered me, thinking I'd be better
off out of the ground. "Why do you think it's a man?"
"Oh honey, it's ALWAYS a man."

My mother sent me underwear after my first divorce.
I was destitute from two years of playing human
punching bag to a man I could never satisfy. She also
sent me hose in a dreadful, not to be mistaken for
human skin tone. Today, while waiting for the
lawyer's call I found four new pairs of panties in the
mailbox. The call came at 7:00. I was on my
own again. I opened a bottle of wine, then another. At
2:00, I was hungry.

"I know all about man problems, that's why I sing the
blues. I can sing 329 songs about being done wrong."
I remember the 283 CD's I have on the shelf at home.
For the last few years, I have only listened to talk-
radio. Mahalia is humming to herself, pausing to
spoon cheese grits onto her tongue. I offer to pay her
check, but she waves the air with a dismissive tone. So
I take the money, stop at the 24-hour Wal-Mart, buy
a Billie Holiday CD, and play it for three days
straight.

Emma's Tattoo

With his fingers tracing lightly across my chest,
he kissed me, stood and adjusted his tie.
Pausing in the doorway, he smiled,
before disappearing down the hall.

On the way to the bathroom,
I stopped in front of the mirror—
Massaging my nipples
between forefinger and thumb
pressing up with my palms,
to create more cleavage.

"This will be uncomfortable," the nurse said.
I willed myself not to scream
when the metal plates pressed,
pressed unmercifully,
until I thought my breasts would explode.

When the technician came
to mark me for radiation
I asked him to make little flowers.
He wouldn't look at me,
"I only have green ink."

Afterwards, the counselor told me not to look.
On the eighth day, after my husband
brought roses, yellow, not red,
I locked myself in the bathroom,
pulled away the bandages, and mourned.

Six months later, I drive
to the outskirts of town
to a rundown store with motorcycles parked in front.
"Yeah, sure honey, no problem,"
the woman wearing a studded leather corset
nods at my drawing of a forget-me-not.
When I pull open my blouse,
the woman with a dragon
climbing from her cleavage,
crosses her arms tight,
stumbles backward, and winces.

Synaesthesia

In a previous life, I was the color orange,
a fact I know because I understand
why it has no rhyme—
a conundrum (a big word,
easy to rhyme) that quality
of warning, inarticulation, defiance,
like Lot's wife, concrete
(which isn't), the Pillars of Hercules
stone fruit, the tower of Babel.
William of Orange was not, so
the Dutch call oranges *sinaasappels*,
meaning Chinese apples,
while most Americans think of Florida
groves which some say are green—
but that is an instance of a very different color.

The Year I Gave Up Elevators

1.
The fog hangs low in the French Quarter,
too early for tourists
still nursing Bourbon Street hangovers.
Alone, I trudge through the alleys
of a city that belonged to two men I love.
They are not waiting for me.
I never saw the New Orleans house.
Yesterday, I ventured as far as their street,
but I couldn't bear seeing the closed door.

2.
Six years ago, when we drove to Florida,
Bill told me his daughter didn't speak to him anymore—
I silently vowed to try to fill that void.
"Don't I give you everything you want?" he asked,
buying me the orange juice with the pour-spout.
I only smiled, thinking, you give me what I need.
I want to go back to that day
walk to the pier, find Bill fishing
help him carry the buckets back to the house,
lounge on the porch with Lamar
while Bill makes lunch.
I want to drink too much at dinner,
sit on the edge of their bed talking
until I can't hold my eyes open.
I want to wake in the morning and
hear them talking softly in the next room.

3.
Last night I walked to Jackson Square,
had my palm read by a man who said
in a past life I was an adventurer,
Amelia Earhart probably. He seemed shocked
by his clairvoyance, when I said
"Amelia and I have the same birthday."
He couldn't divine the answer I came for,
Why have these two men disappeared from my life?

4.
I wander into the church
Just across from where I had my palm read.
Inside a group of nuns is saying the Rosary.
It is the fifth Saturday of Lent—
this year I gave up elevators.
If Christ could walk to Calvary
I figured I could take the stairs.
I wonder if Amelia gave up flying
just at the moment she disappeared?
I pray for the sick, for my soul, light a candle
sprinkle Holy water on my forehead.
On my way back to the hotel, I stop at a salon
tell the guy to cut my hair—short.

5.
Back at the Atlanta airport
I bump into old friends,
who tell me about another death.
I steady myself against the baggage cart,
not sure I can stand the weight—
so much death,
the stairs I've yet to climb.

Confessions of a Shelter Volunteer

Everything I say is a lie:
"We have just what you need.
Help is on the way.
You'll get through this."
Empty platitudes beside
        my overpaid for retro sneakers,
        my designer name peasant shirt,
        my fashionably distressed jeans.
I offer up miniature soaps & mouthwash,
the kind I steal on vacations, but never use.
I sort foul industrial linens,
register people too tired to speak,
hold babies while their mothers cry.
        My goal is to help—
a cliché that sinks quickly
in a sea of non-language
where all the possessive
words have drowned.
Tonight, I will feather-pillow dream
        my lies
in the only world where they can be true.

Georgia Seasonal

Summer

Peaches and muscadines
fill the baskets at roadside stands.
Slippery slices of sunrise flesh,
tart envy-green Concord cousins,
pressed into homemade vintage
only a July tongue could savor—
Sugared moonshine to cool humid afternoons
passed on Saturday porches,
not mentioned on Sunday benches.

Autumn

The explosions sweep southward,
red and gold flame bursts
ignite the Appalachian Trail.
Nature's Joshua through the Blue Ridge,
down along the shores of the Chattahoochee,
until all that's left north of Atlanta
are gangly Georgia pines, green in defiance,
needles like phoenix tail-feathers
shivering in the sorghum scented air.

Winter

Nothing really dies here.
Even roses bloom in the mild years,
and we Southerners become smug about our home.
Yet, the cornhusks were thick at harvest,
the wooly worms are dense with fur.
The natives know the penance for
too much comfort, expect ice this year,
know that resurrection requires suffering, death.

Spring

Monet's Giverny has nothing on Atlanta—
like lily pads, the kudzu floats on red clay,
verdant quick cover spreading feet per day,
until the background is set, dark and lush,
for white mountain laurel, pink rhododendron,
wild orange-blaze azalea, and blue hydrangea.
Dogwoods blooming blood-edged Christ petals,
magnolia blossoms cup baptismal rain.

Inclement

This morning cold rain bullets pierce my skin,
Still, it's a relief from thirty-seven inches of snow,
and windchills lower than grade school children can
        count—
minus twenty, minus warmth, dead feet and hands.
When I left the South, a friend gave me a copy of
        Springsteen's *Nebraska*—
about Starkweather, blustering hometown killer
buried in the cemetery three blocks from where I live.
I long for home, temperate Georgia,
where my winter coat is the stranger at the door.

Estate Sale
Palm Sunday, Lincoln, NE

More than a hundred people trampled the newly
greening yard, pawing at the items lining tables,
stacked on the ground, even hanging from tree limbs.
Her name is Mary; she just moved to a nursing home.
My friend bought a chair—a regal scalloped back
number in gold crushed velvet. Only fifty cents. I
picture Miss Mary perched on the edge of that chair,
in the front room on Sundays, drinking coffee with
friends and family. Where are they now? I think about
skipping Mass—the palm fronds, Jesus entering
Jerusalem in triumph, only a few days from his
crucifixion. I begin bidding against everyone, driving
up prices, leave with three Japanese stamp prints in
decaying frames. Thirty-two dollars.

Abortive Midnight Journal Entry
after Everette Maddox

Here in Nebraska, I am buried
under snow and self-pity.
If only you weren't buried too,
we could consult your dictionary—
look for words that mean something—
toast my newest job rejection letter.
The reward for having advanced
education is not employment—
at least not the paying kind.
Days like this, I want to drift
down to the Maple Leaf Bar—
drink Louisiana humidity,
thickened gin cotton-coating
my throat, until the slow burn
erases all thoughts of poetry.

Ice Storm

A difficult beauty is in it
the inch of sheer water
glistening in twilight
as if weightless—
the collapse imminent.

Something of a shot rings out.
A branch claws its way down,
grasping the power
lines into darkness.

I watch from the window-seat.
A worker steers his cherry-picker,
deus ex machina,
toward the main transformer.

He hauls up guide-wires
his shadow chorus, eyes heavenward,
moving *strophe* and *antistrophe*,
until the sudden reconnection—
the blinding light.

Aeolian Intercession

The high-stress fishing line
tied with a human knot
bows to the wind's will
loosing its grip on the hollow
Applewood wind-chimes.
After the crash,
the patio palm plant, silent and alone,
prays for the return of music.

In Lithuania, the Hill of Crosses,
(bulldozed three times in the Cold War)
resurrected, watches over Siauliai
where the wind fingers
millions of rosaries, patiently listens.
From a distance you hear it—
Vespers from rattled wood, metal, plastic—
prayer for what cannot be destroyed.

Lepidoptera
Sewanee, July 2002

The ceremony of moths had stopped us
thousands of them swarming in the heat
of spot lights on a too tall memorial
cross, and when we slammed on the brakes, just short,
the wind released our hair and the moths came,
circled, and lit safely on our bodies
fluttered on our eyelashes and eardrums,
breath-like, cool and alive in the darkness.
To say we were like moths seems cliché,
yet there we were, much too old for midnight
fast drives with the rag top down, rebelling
against a misplaced sense of our lost youth
on that mountain pass, nothing but gravel
and guardrail between the North Star and us—

IV

"I was blessed with humble beginnings."
—Dolly Parton

Instructions for My Burial Clothes

Sometimes I dream
Dolly Parton is my aunt.
I'm about twelve.
She comes to visit
at Easter,
brings me chocolates,
jelly beans
and makeup.

My mother frowns,
hurries around the kitchen
with other female relatives—
they are all wearing sackcloth.
Dolly sits beside me,
plays a guitar and sings,
her long red-glittered nails
click against the frets.

When I say,
"Do not bury me in a suit,
I want to go out in sequins,"
my mother shakes her head,
wonders where I learned such excess.

Author's Note

Poems in section II have titles in common with popular songs. These poems are part of a series of semi-autobiographical poems and the titles reflect the #1 song from the week of my birth for several years of my life.

Acknowledgements

Breathing the Same Air: An Anthology of East Tennessee Writers: Ella's Diner

Burnside Review: The One that You Love

Chattahoochee Review: On Visiting Duane Allman's Grave

Knoxville Bound: A Literary Anthology: Southern Girls

Mid-America Poetry Review: Exhibitions

New Millennium Writings: Southern Gothic, Still Life

O' Georgia: An Anthology of Georgia's Newest and Most Promising Writers: Legacy

Ordinary Review: Part of the Bargain

Plain Song Review: Estate Sale

Prairie Schooner: Annie's Song, Georgia Clay, Grandmother's Spit, The Hustle, Living in the Material World, It's Still Rock and Roll to Me

ReDactions: Instructions for My Burial Clothes

Solo Cafe: Confessions of a Shelter Volunteer

Southeast Review: Emma's Tattoo

Umpteen Ways of Looking at a Possum: Creative & Critical Responses to Everette Maddox: Abortive Midnight Journal Entry

War, Literature, and the Arts: An International Journal of the Humanities: Bad Girls, Miltary Wife

The Women's Review of Books Hester Speaks, Indian Reservation

Special thanks to the *James and Mary Wesley Center for New Media*, the *School of Literature, Communication, and Culture*, and the *Center for the Enhancement of Teaching and Learning* at *Georgia Tech* for supporting my work.

My deepest gratitude to Colin Potts, Grace Bauer, Hilda Raz, Greg Kuzma, Ted Kooser, Randall Snyder, Caroline Noyes, Art Smith, Collin Kelley, Rupert Fike, Liz Ahl, Tom Lux, Kurt Brown, Linda Pratt, Donna Llewellyn, Tom Williams, Bob Kunzinger, my friends, my family, and to the NDYPs (Blake Leland, JC Reilly, and Bob Wood) for reading, critiquing, or otherwise supporting this project.

In fond remembrance of Oyekan Owomoyela.

About the Author

Karen Head is the author of *My Paris Year* (All Nations Press, 2009) and *Shadow Boxes* (All Nations Press, 2003). Her poetry appears, or is forthcoming, in a number of national and international journals and anthologies, and has been invited to present her work in the U.S. and Europe. As a scholar of contemporary American poetry, she has begun to explore the connections between traditional text-based poetry and digitally-enhanced poetry, an exploration that involves her in a number of creative projects being conducted in the Wesley Center for New Media at Georgia Tech. Her first digital poetry project, *Poetic Rub*, was featured at the E-Poetry 2007 festival in Paris. Head is the Graduate Communication Coordinator and Special Advisor to the Writing and Communication Program at Georgia Tech. Additionally she serves on the Poetry Atlanta Board, a non-profit organization dedicated to supporting poets and promoting poetry in the Atlanta area. She founded and is developing *The Peachtree Review* as a venue for both traditional and digital poetry.